What to expect when expecting a law enforcement promotional process

By

Nicholas Ruggiero

ISBN:9798489762205

Dedication

First and foremost this book is dedicated to you. Without your support my books would fall on deaf ears and the movement would die. Folks like you and I are the hard workers in law enforcement that get fed crumbs and when we ask for more are punished. I hope you knock the process out of the park and infiltrate the command staff in your agency. Remember, don't forget where you came from and mentor future leaders.

To my wife who always encourages my ventures and is my biggest fan. You always see the best in me when I don't and always make me realize my potential. I love you.

Hailey and Emily, I love you so much and I hope you achieve everything in your life that you set out for. You both are amazing and very loved.

To my Mom, A warrior in sheep's clothes and always there for me. My Mom wanted to be a writer when she was a kid and being able to do it as her son continues her legacy. These past few months I couldn't have made it without you.

TJ, Laura, and Alex I love you guys. Marco & Andrea are the realist people in Virginia and I truly believe part of our family. Logan you are amazing! Ernie thank you for always checking on me and being my test subject on my books. Rene N, bro I can't tell you how becoming friends is something I cherish. I looked up to you coming up and to have your approval on these books means the world.

Heather from Rocks for LEO's thank you for being a good friend. Ed thank you for "Bro time" filled with cigars, coffee, and laughs. You're a mentor and someone I value as a friend. Mike, Michael, Joe, and that woman you're married to thank you for being our family and being my ride or die. Mike I'm hoping the gender surgery is a success, No one should judge you for doing what makes you comfortable. Barclay for always being a good friend and great leader. Joe Smarro, "I see you" brother! Thank you for everything you do for LE.

To the commanders, supervisors, and officers from my old agency stuck on retaliation. Your time will come and when karma takes it's course I hope you're strong enough to navigate through it. Watching that place destroy itself from the inside makes me giggle every day.

In memory of Mr. Whiting

A man of honor, integrity, and devotion to his family and friends. Father of Bart Whiting a fellow LEO and someone I consider a good friend. Your dad helped me in times when I was the lowest. He was a guardian angel and will be missed.

Foreword

Alexandria, Virginia is a small metropolis located just outside the District of Washington. A city, outside, the city with a general population of approximately 150,000 residents on a given night or weekend and as much as 500,000 people during a normal workday. Demographics range from both sides of the spectrum from inner city living conditions to a small neighborhood nicknamed "Beverly Hills;" crime equally on both sides as well- from a barking dog complaint to your vicious homicide. The local police department consists of roughly 350 sworn members and of that, 150, on a good night, assigned to the patrol division.

Our unit, although assigned to patrol, had a unique design. We were aptly called the Power Shift, not for what you would think, but we were a permanently scheduled shift of evening officers that worked a set schedule of days on and days off. We were a very close-knit group of officers, and in charge of it all was Sergeant Nicholas Ruggiero.

Nick was five academy classes before mine, and as officers we shared a unique bond from the moment we met. Both from New York, we already had a few things in common, but after my first run in with the leadership of our department over my marriage, and Nick's issue with the same leadership after a pursuit, we became even closer. We were the bastard children of the department. Two strong, opinionated, people who felt that they were being treated differently than any other officer.

Nick put in for the rank of Sergeant long before I ever considered the idea. I recall asking him why he wanted to at such an early stage in his career as doing so clearly wasn't for any financial purposes...and he stated that he wanted to make a difference, and that the current leadership was tainted with cliques and the buddy system. If you wanted to implement any change, you are just going to have to do it yourself. So, he did, and scored high.

As a Sergeant on the Power Shift, and my current assignment as a School Resource Officer going back to patrol, Nick requested and basically went to bat for me to get placed on his squad. As I was still dealing with my own issues with the current leadership, I eventually was granted the position. I would have to say that of all the Sergeants I have been assigned to, Nick was one of the most reasonable and fair supervisors in my career. His ability to not only lead the squad to any given objective, but he was also always right there along side you. Even when he exited that the sewer drainpipe in the middle of the night after a pursuit and fell into the small ravine right outside wearing not only his full duty gear, but a nice cardigan sweater in the middle of a Northern Virginia winter. Standing there with this look like a scene from the movie "It" .... the only thing missing was the red balloon, and a pair of water wings which later became the joke of the squad.

So, when Nick asked me to write the forward to his latest book, I was taken aback as to why. What did I have to contribute to his success in this book? So, I began to do a little research and from not only my own personal experiences as a leader both in law enforcement but also in the military, I realized I might have some perspective.

So, what is leadership?

According to Forbes magazine, leadership is a process of social influence, which maximizes the efforts of others, towards the achievement of a goal.

Notice key elements of this definition:

- Leadership stems from *social* influence, not authority or power
- Leadership requires others, and that implies they don't need to be "direct reports"
- No mention of personality traits, attributes, or even a title; there are many styles, many paths, to effective leadership
- It includes *a goal*, not influence with no intended outcome

Lastly, what makes this definition so different from many of the academic definitions out there is the inclusion of "maximizes the efforts".

This definition clearly reminded me of Nick's style of leadership which aligns much with my own. I will never ask a subordinate to perform a task that I myself, would not be willing to do. I would always encourage growth in my people and listen to their ideas. Place value onto others as I myself can learn from others at any time.

Even after all our Roll Call Room podcasts, where we demean leadership and condemn those in it within our old department, Nick has a solid understanding of what a leader is supposed to be. Not only did he approach every promotional exam with optimism, but he did it with a purpose. Not for recognition, not for pay, but to effect change…to effect moral of others.

Many promotional processes are very textbook, “leave no child behind” mentalities. Most accommodate everyone, and that’s fine...but take the process for the right reasons. You are the ones who people will look up to for answers, direction, support. You are their network, just because you have a different title, know what is truly expected from you, what is needed!!

I would follow Nick’s orders with little to no questions asked, because I know Nick’s character, I know Nick. I don’t expect special treatment, I will do my job and expect a fair evaluation. So, if I can give any advice, knowing where Nick comes from, this book is about the realities of being a leader, not just the privileges of the rank.

Table of Contents

CHAPTER 1

Making the decision

So you've made the decision to leap into the law enforcement ranks? Don't take this decision too lightly and I hope you're doing it for the right reasons.

Leadership in law enforcement has over the past few decades destroyed moral and caused the worst recruiting problem in history. Those "leaders" probably had the best intentions like you when they decided to prepare for the promotional process. Some were really horrible street cops but incredible at taking promotional processes. That or they have incredibly great knees and joints to cushion multiple impacts to the throat.

In all seriousness making the decision to take a promotional process is a big one. The commitment you'll need for this process is critical. You'll need extreme discipline for studying and memorization. While your competitors are focused on department policy and trying to out smart the process you'll need to trust this process.

Your focus should be on thinking outside the box and not like a cop. Yea, you heard me right. Every answer during your process requires articulation of each STEP in detail like you're explaining it to a class of high school students.

If you follow the instructions and utilize the writing exercises I'm going to supply you with it will elevate your chances of being selected for a promotion or specialized unit. How do I know? I've helped in my former agency over 40 people get promoted or selected for specialized units. Every promotional process has the same goal; identify the best candidate through a series of questions, practicals, and/or panels. If you surrender you skepticism and follow what I lay out you will be able to achieve your goal of promotion or appointment to the unit you choice.

Now… I can't control the horse trading behind closed doors in your department. If your department holds promotional processes sacred and promote based off of published scores than its imperative that you achieve every point available for each portion of the process.

That being said, let's get this show on the road and dive right into it!

CHAPTER 2

"Thinking outside the box"

We hear all the time in law enforcement to "think outside the box" but in a promotional process it has a different meaning. The term in a promotional process means to think about all the options, units, toys, and resources available to you that the typical person wouldn't think about.

If I asked you this practice question what would your five minute answer be? *"A call just came out at 1434hrs that a robbery at the local 7-11 just occurred. The suspect was armed and fired a round striking the clerk in the arm and fled on the interstate in a white Nissan Altima missing one hubcap. Evening shift comes into roll call at 1530hrs."*

Ok. What did you come up with? Now the typical answers apply like; ensure at least two officers are responding, have medics stage, ensure you head to the call as a supervisor or commander, put a bolo out for the vehicle, have the first unit secure the crime scene, and preserve evidence.

This question is a great example of what resources are available at your finger tips but during a process aren't utilized. This costs you points and shows that you're not detail oriented. Don't worry! I got your six and I'm about to blow your mind.

Every question during a process has a beginning, middle, and an end. Where most candidates go wrong is they don't end the question. I'll explain in a bit what I mean. The start of every scenario is to access where your heads at. How you organize your resources and how you command a scene. Let's take the sample question. It's 1443hrs, almost every person is working in your department. Everyone from the Chief (I hope) all the way down to crossing guards. When you run a scene for these processes every resources is available to you.

For the sample question; dispatch motors unit to set up perimeter, dispatch detectives to the scene to start the investigation, dispatch K9 to the scene to start a track for possible evidence left by suspect, notify the evenings Sergeant to call the shift in early and hit the street with no roll call, if your department has a helicopter get it in the air or ask for mutual aid for one, notify state police to set up a perimeter on the interstate, have a unit establish a perimeter with crime scene tape, CLOSE THE BUSINESS, contact the watch commander, PIO, or what's required in your department policy, notify the nearest school to lock down, once the scene is secured render aid to the clerk and assign an officer to accompany him/her to the hospital and instruct the officer to provide updates on condition, secure witness statements and contact information, and have an officer canvas for video.

Did you hit any of these? If so, you're on the right path. If not, don’t worry I’ll get you there. The examples I just laid out will elevate you to the next level because you’re thinking outside the box.

We’ve got everyone in place and utilizing a good amount of resources. We need to start to de-escalate the scene. You need to remember who you called in, who you alerted, who’s on a holding pattern, who’s on overtime, and in what order to take things down.

Start with the most biggest fiscal impact to the agency. If you put a bird in the air, get that cleared (fuel is expensive). The choice to clear the school lock down before you release motors is another major attention to detail. If you release motors first and then open school the traffic is going to be chaotic, a traffic hazard, and may cause a bus of kids to get injured. You need to verbalize this rationalization! DETAIL!

With any process if you don't say it, it didn't happen. You're talking to panel of cops but these folks can't give you credit for things until you verbalize it. I call this process diarrhea of the mouth. You should be spitting out everything and anything to keep them writing. We'll get into time management and observation of observers later in this book.

Ok, so we've started to calm things down in our scenario and now we need to make notifications. Part of being a supervisor or commander is letting everyone know what's going on. That means a call, text, email, or alert. You have to remember to verbalize that you'll do all of these each step of the scenario. Notifications are key because executive staff or your politicians running your city, town, or county have to be in the know. They like to be part of the cool kids and like alerts. Makes them feel important which we all know….

We have a beginning, we've started to break down the scene and slowly turn everything over to the Dick Tracy crew, but we have a major responsibility that most candidates forget when taking a process which is ending it right. If during my sample you just ended it by shutting the scene down and calling it a day this next part is important. Here's the next part sample:

After breaking down the scene I would hold a debriefing. At the debriefing I would ensure everyone have the case number and proper title for the report. I would hand out overtime slips and ensure they are completed and signed. I would check all reports for accuracy and submit them. I would offer EAP or peer support for anyone that needs it during my debriefing. Ensure the victim in the case has been offered services and the business owner if offered any crime prevention options available through the department. I would complete an after action memorandum detailing the incident and our response, services, and area we can improve on. I would ensure that patrol units are proactively patrolling that 7-11 and checking in with the business.

That attention to detail at the end of the scenario is almost as important as what you're doing during it. It's the difference between being in the middle of the pack of candidates or leading it. Almost everyone forgets to check reports, overtime slips, and after action report. These are things that we do every time but we don't verbalize it during a process. If you don't say it, it didn't happen!

FOLLOW UP! Every question during a promotional process requires follow up. I like to do a 30,60,90 approach. This is your follow up pattern. At the end of each question say, "I'd follow up every 30,60, and 90 days". Follow up is that last piece to show your attention to detail and that you're committed to resolving whatever the issue is.

The people that put these processes together have no idea that we don't have time for half this stuff but they want to hear it. Remember, almost half of promotional processes within law enforcement are written by outside companies with almost zero input by your agency or law enforcement. A lot of the scenarios are current event driven. That means you can almost predict what some of your scenarios will be based on the current events within society. In the 90's it was about the drug wars, late 90's early 00's was community policing, and currently its about use of force, de-escalation, internal investigations, civilian oversight, and school's.

You should be brainstorming about your answers to these current topics within law enforcement. Your answers should be tailored towards appeasing citizens while adhering to department policy.

In your answers dealing with any citizen complaint, civilian oversight, or community policing you should be offering things like a ride along, citizen academy, and citizen review board if your department has it. Talk about attending HOA meetings or civic association meetings to educate the public. Utilize your departments social media or email list.

These are the things that will set you apart from the other candidates. Most of us in law enforcement go into promotional processes thinking that you just need to answer the questions directly, get in and get out. This is a major mistake. You need to think outside the box and have attention to detail.

CHAPTER 3

Time Management

One of the most important things in taking a process is to manage your time. NEVER EVER give back time. What do I mean? If you have five minutes to answer a questions, take the full five minutes. In this chapter I'm going to go over a few techniques that can help you during the timed portion of the process.

In a lot of these processes you'll have a timed portion where your time management and prioritizing skills are put to test. They literally tell you have much time you have. In some cases they'll say, "This portion is six questions and you have 30 minutes to answer." You should be writing this down if they supplied scrap paper. Do the math and you'll determine that you have five minutes per question.

The moment the first question is read to your provided to you write down the time. Keep yourself on task by adhering to the last chapter about attention to detail. When you're finished with a train of thought look at your watch. At the end of the first question write the end time. If you went over five minutes make sure you manage your time and shave off the time over.

If you get a brain fart and stall out ask to have the question read to you again. If the questions are provided on paper read it out loud. Embarrassing yes but its a physiological technique to spark information from your brain. Your brain needs a stimulus of information to jump start it. You'd be surprised that just having the question being read to you or you reading it out loud will spark that diarrhea of the mouth I spoke about in the last chapter.

In the scenario based portion of your promotional process time management is extremely critical. You need to be precise on your management of time. The management of time can be mastered through practice scenarios and recording yourself while studying. We'll go over this technique in the book.

I want you to get into the mindset that the time limit is YOUR time. Don't give back any time during this process. Where candidates go wrong is that they come out the gate with a ton of information and think that they got it all and they didn't. It's always in the middle of the next question that they say, "Shit, I forgot to say…..". Don't be that candidate. Be systematic and methodical in your answers. If you follow the first chapter and have a beginning, middle, and an end to each scenario or question then you shouldn't have an "oh shit" moment.

That's why its very important that you take the time to do the practice exercises and time your responses. Recording your practice is also a great way to see what five minutes looks like. When you play back your answers you'll hear yourself stutter or pause during brain gaps. You'll actually hear when your brain is trying to pull for answers but comes up empty handed. This will be eliminated with practice and training your brain to draw from a bag of new resources. By running these exercises over and over some of these outside of the box resources will become second nature and part of muscle memory. Just like working with your firearm you'll be able to react naturally and like second nature.

CHAPTER 4

Preparing/Studying

Studying for a process is a process all in it self. Everyone has their own technique and if yours works for you then stick with it. This chapter is to give you some ideas and statistical data on how study patterns help or hurt your end goal.

Tip 1: Space out your studying. It's important for you to space out your study pattern and not suffer from study fatigue. Fight the urge to study everyday for hours at a time. This will only cause your brain to shut of memorizing and switch to coasting.

This is a common mistake by candidates for promotional processes. You think by studying constantly and for countless hours is dedication and a sign of commitment to the rank you're trying to achieve. It's commendable but not necessary.

Tip 2: Create a study calendar. In this book you'll get the tips and tricks but ultimately learning your departments policies and procedures lands on your shoulders. Every department (I hope) has a binder full of general orders or policies. Trying to study and memorize them is a beast.

Set yourself a study calendar of core directives to study and specifically the supervisor or commander responsibility portion. These core directives should be Use if force, Investigations, Evidence, Domestics, Death cases, Biased policing, Community Policing, Civil Disobedience, Critical Incidents, FEMA, Sexual harassment, and internal investigations.

I’m not saying only those policies but these are the core policies that get people fired or are routinely issues for law enforcement. You need to know as a supervisor or commander how to navigate through these issues.

Your study calendar should not be five policies a day to memorize. You should set a goal of one a day. Yes, one a day to read, comprehend, and be able to articulate your role.

Your study calendar should factor in practicals at the end of the week. Use the practice scenarios supplied in this book at the end of every study week. Record each one and listen to them on your car ride in or while you're working. Listen to the progression of your skills get better. Are you getting better at articulating your responses? Adjust your study pattern as your progress.

Tip 3: 2hr rule. You should set your daily training for 2hrs maximum. Fight the urge to have all night or all morning study sessions. Trust me, it may seem like you're getting a lot in doing six hours of studying but in reality you're not.

After 2hrs the brain is done. It's slowly slipping into coasting mode like we spoke about before. Don't over work your brain or piss it off. Be kind to it and give him/ her a break.

Tip 4: PRACTICE! I can't stress this enough and I'll say it a ton in this book. Practice makes perfect! I've seen a lot of shit heads get promoted based strictly on how they practiced scenarios over and over to the point that they had it as second nature.

You can’t just read the scenarios in this book and say, “Yea I’d do X,Y, and Z”. You need to record yourself saying what you would do in chronological order. When you play it back listen to yourself. Did you explain things in a precise definitive manner? Did you have a begging, middle, and end? Did you follow up at the end?

Practice the scenarios! When you have it down, practice again.

Tip 5: Get rest. This is a tough one for cops. Your brain functions at its highest when it has rest. You need to disconnect from studying and let your brain absorb the knowledge that you're dropping into it. Don’t study before bed each night either. This will only make you analyze what you’ve studied and cause your brain to work overtime when it should be resting.

On the day before the process do NOTHING. You've done everything you can do and have confidence in what you put into getting ready. Cramming the night before is not the answer. The night before you should be focused on making sure your dress attire is locked in and spending time with your family. Yes, being nervous is natural and not at all a sign that you're not ready. You need to have confidence!

Tip 6: Day of process ritual. Again, this is not the time to be study cramming. I've taken a lot of processes and have seen candidates sitting in their cars or hiding in the locker room with papers all over the place like its tax season. WRONG! If you stuck to the study calendar and utilized what's in this book then you're as ready as you're going to be.

You need to eat breakfast. I am the biggest anti breakfast person and even I need to concede that there is a science behind it. Don't down a Monster drink and jerky as breakfast. The last thing you need is an energy drink to raise you up and crash in the middle of the process. Yes, coffee is good but in conjunction with an actual breakfast.

Brain food is a real thing folks. These are foods that have been proven to help with brain health. What are some good brain foods?

- Blueberries
- Eggs
- Fruits
- Leafy greens
- Nuts
- Pumpkin seeds
- Tea and Coffee

- Whole grains

From personal experience I always do oatmeal with blueberries with coffee. Just before I start the process I down a banana and have enough fuel to get me over the finish line. Do research and fine a good food to have the morning of the process.

CHAPTER 5

Conflict resolution practical

Almost always a promotional process will test your skills on dealing with internal conflicts. No, not dealing with fights with yourself. These are conflicts that you will encounter with your staff or superior(s).

Any conflict that you have must be resolved in a satisfactory manner that is within department policy and adheres to labor laws, collective bargaining agreements, and municipality policy. It's in your best interest to brush up on these policies.

One of the leading factors that cost cops their jobs is domestic violence and fraternization. Knowing how to navigate through those land mines as a supervisor or commander is key. Your fuck up can cost the agency and municipality a lot of money. So this is a key thing most processes test on.

So, the following question is a sample of what may be asked of you during the process. **You have five minutes to answer this question:**

"While in your office you hear Officer Jones making comments to a female officer. These jokes are in a sexual manner and loud enough to be heard by several people getting ready for roll call. Officer Jones is currently on a Performance Improvement Plan (PIP) for the same type of incident less than two months ago. What as his supervisor is your plan of action?"

This is a tough one right? Not really when you take it apart. The bottom line is that you must adhere to your policy and be fair and impartial. As a supervisor or commander you can or will definitely encounter this very scenario.

Let's break down some detailed outside of the box thinking answers.

- Immediately take action by separating both parties.
- Advise your supervisor of the incident immediately and document the date and time.
- Have the female officer choose a fellow officer to sit with while you take further action.
- Notify Internal Investigations
- Notify Human Resources
- Review Officer Jones' file and confirm the date and time of the previous PIP.
- Provide Mr. Jones with his Garrity rights (If your department has collective bargaining.

- Advise the other Sergeant/Watch Commander that all three officers will not attend roll call and possibly need coverage for the shift.
- Determine if video or audio of the comment is available (Body camera footage or CCTV). If body camera is in place within your agency, immediately download buffer footage.
- Secure a statement from Officer Jones including acknowledgment of prior counseling.
- Offer EAP, Peer support, and/or mental health services to Officer Jones.
- Interview and secure a statement from the female officer without the peer officer in the room.
- Offer the female officer EAP, Peer support, and/or mental health services.
- Provide an option for the officer to go home without utilizing her leave. If she accepts, offer a ride home.

- Partner with your supervisor, HR, and possibly the Chief or Sheriff to issue administrative leave for Officer Jones.
- Get the restrictions for administrative leave ie: Gun, badge, and credentials surrendered.
- Offer a peer of Officer Jones to accompany him and you to change out for the night.
- Access Officer Jones' mental state during this process. Does Officer Jones pose a threat to himself or others? If yes, take action immediately by securing his weapon and EAP, peer support, or mental health assessment is no longer an option, its a requirement that must be documented on any administrative leave or suspension paperwork and as a condition of his employment.
- Look at the duty roster for the shift and begin to secure possible witness statements.

- Ensure that any leave slips are signed by both officers prior to them leaving.
- Follow up with each officer that night and ensure that they arrived safe at home and answer any questions you can without compromising the investigation
- Complete an accurate and detailed memorandum including statements, recordings, video, and copies of the prior PIP. This memorandum should document dates and times.
- Follow up with your supervisor/commander on a report back date for the female officer. Upon her return debrief and ensure that she is mentally fit for duty. If so, follow up through out the shift and ensure that any questions or services she needs are met. Document efforts.

- Follow up with Internal Investigations, HR, and command staff for Officer Jones' status. Ensure that he is updated according to department policy.
- Document your follow up following the incident and utilize your after action report for any future similar cases you may have.

Did you get these? What did your response look like? Were you focused on just documenting it and moving on? Did you utilize resources for both parties? FOLLOW UP?

It's easy to steer off on something like this scenario, but it's really simple. Party A did something to Party B and against department policy. Your main job is to gather facts. Just like out on the street you are a fact finder. Your job is to give the female officer the best investigation you can so that she knows the department and you take it seriously. In the same breath you owe it to Officer Jones to give him a fair and unbiased investigation. A past violation is just a snippet of the totality of the current incident.

As supervisor/commander you're not either persons buddy. You need to remain fair and display that in the process.

Now more than ever supervisors/commanders need to be focused on mental health. You should be thinking about services like EAP, Peer support, and/or Mental health services. This can have a tremendous impact on the people that work for you. Don't leave your people in the cold especially when they are put of administrative leave. That's a major stressor for officers and you don't know how they'll react. You need to ask, "Are you thinking about hurting yourself?". Say it in the process!

I can't stress this enough, Follow up every time. You have a tremendous amount of things that need to be followed up on with this scenario.

CHAPTER 6

Sample questions &

Practicals

Please explain what you have done in the past to prepare yourself for a managerial position (Job, situations, education, training, etc.).

Please explain what attributes you possess that will allow you to be a successful Sergeant or commander within (Insert your agency name) (Study the announcement).

As a Sergeant, one of your charges approaches you before roll call and advises you that he is having problems at home which is affecting his performance at work…how would you handle this situation?

As a sergeant, one of your officer is continuously arriving for work late...you had an initial meeting with him/her but this does not seem to remedy the situation, how would handle this situation?

Two of your officers were called to Applebees because the manager called about a customer who was observed carrying a pistol attached to his belt… officers respond…ask the customer to come out of the restaurant …disarm the customer and ask the customer to identify himself and complete an information card…the customer complained about the entire incident and requested for a supervisor to respond…upon arriving on the scene and learning the above facts…what would you do and explain any steps taken after customer leaves.

As a midnight Supervisor within patrol, you receive numerous complaints regarding (Insert a local trouble address). Citizens are complaining that they see persons coming in and out of the house at all hours of the night and that they only stay for five minutes at a time...they believe the occupants of the house are dealing drugs...explain how you would handle the situation as a PATROL SERGEANT or COMMANDER.

A subject was observed forcing a woman into a vehicle at (Insert an address in your jurisdiction)...a lookout was posted...approximately 10 minutes later...the same vehicle was observed parked on the side of the road, unoccupied, on the parkway approximately ½ mile north of the city line...the interior is bloodied...as on scene supervisor...how would you handle the scene?

As a sergeant, one of your officers advises you that Ofc. Smith, for the past two weeks, appears lethargic, is having problems at home, and does not appear to be engaging with other officers or citizens while out on the streets, how would you handle this situation?

DOOMSDAY SCENARIO

(This scenario will evolve and progress. Handle this scenario with that in mind)

A call for service goes out indicating the Wendy's was just robbed by two subjects armed with guns… unknown if subjects still on scene…with the duty roster in hand…respond to the location and take the necessary steps to manage scene…

Approx. 20 minutes after determining the suspects were no longer on scene at the Wendy's... Communications receives a call stating two suspects matching suspects' descriptions were seen running east on the road three blocks from the Wendy's...as the supervisor who is still at the Wendy's...what would you do?

Officer Smith transmits on the radio that he has one suspect in view. As he calls out the subject stop you hear gun shots and yelling. The dispatcher attempts to raise Officer Smith with no success. Officer Smith is not answering his radio. What is your next move?

You arrive at the scene of Officer Smith's shooting and observe spectators forming and growing. The scene is becoming hostile and your staffing is now stretched thin. The press is now arriving on scene. What are your next steps?

As your securing the scene the family of the suspect arrives on scenes and sees the suspect deceased on the floor and attempts to break through the crime scene. Officer Smith is still on scene and experiencing shock and struggling to maintain his composure. What's your next step?

After you are relieved from the scene and return back to headquarters what are your next steps?

CHAPTER 7
RESOURCES

Now comes fine-tuning your responses to those scenarios. These resources are a good way to help you elevate your score by utilizing things other candidates wouldn't even think of. Use them properly and at the right time. Remember what you used so you can de-escalate at the end of your scenario.

- Day Patrol
- Evening Patrol
- Midnight Patrol
- Detectives
- Parking enforcement
- School Resource Officers
- Crossing Guards
- Motors
- Street Crimes
- Vice/Narcotics
- Community Police
- Crime Prevention

- Human Resources
- Internal Investigations
- Citizens Academy
- Youth Academy
- Civilian Review Board
- District Attorney/Commonwealth Attorney/ Magistrate/Public Defenders Office
- Probation and Parole
- Marshalls, DEA, ATF, FBI, Homeland Security, Federal resources
- State Police
- Task Forces
- Crime analysis
- K9
- Air unit/Drones
- Social Media
- Public Information Officer
- Cadet program/Auxiliary unit
- Sheriff's Department, Local Police, Mutual Aid
- Federal Grants
- State Grants
- Harbor Unit

- Media
- Incident Command (ICS)
- EAP, CISM, CIT, Peer Support, other services
- Victim Services
- Domestic violence resources
- Sexual Assault services
- Juvenile services
- Court services
- Protective order/restraining order
- Fiscal Management
- CSI
- Crash investigations unit
- Clergy
- City, County, Village, Town officials
- Code enforcement
- Fire Department/Medics
- Fire Marshal
- SWAT/Fugitive apprehension unit
- Tax records
- NCIC
- LINX
- Department information database

- Criminal History
- AFIS
- CODUS
- Cell phone GPS track or "Ping"
- Amber alert
- Silver alert
- Code ADAM
- Security for property of scene or incident
- CCTV
- Medical release form
- Workers Compensation
- Employee personnel file and next of kin information
- After action report
- Campus Police/Public safety
- FEMA
- Red Cross
- Homeless shelter
- Adult protective services
- Child protective services
- Animal control
- Game warden

- Parks and Forestry
- Arborist
- Electric, Gas, and other utilities
- Local transit (This is great for situations where weather effects your scene; Utilize a public or school bus as a warming or cooling station for people on scene or victims)
- Airports
- Onstar, Lojack, or other vehicle services
- Crime scene clean up or fire department to hose down a scene after processing.
- Wrecker services
- DOT & DOT placard resources for hazardous material.
- Substance abuse services
- Department of Health, CDC, WHO
- Tip line, Crime stoppers, and other lead resources
- US Border Patrol
- TSA
- US Customs
- US Military (MP's, JAG, etc)
- National Weather Service
- National Oceanic and Atmospheric Administration

These resources are not the only resources available but are some that most candidates forget.

CHAPTER 8
REVIEW

How'd you do? These scenarios are designed to get you to think outside the box and utilize resources that you commonly wouldn't think of.

The start of most processes are soft questions. These questions will test your preparation for the promotion like, "What have you done to prepare for this position?". These are soft balls but if you don't get detailed in your answers then it's an easy strike out.

Remember at the start of the book we discussed panel members? These folks were asked to participate in these processes to evaluate each candidate fairly and unbiased. Even though some if not all of them are law enforcement when they walk in to do evaluations they are no longer law enforcement. They have zero training and experience about law enforcement during the evaluation. You need to be aware that you are basically talking to civilians and need to paint a big picture for them. You need to drive in fine details and the "why" of what we do. The panel accessors aren't going to give you sympathy credit or say to themselves, "I know what he/she is trying to explain". They will only give you credit for what you say and not what you meant to say or trying to say.

I've sat on many promotional process panels and it's frustrating to see someone spinning their wheels trying to explain what they mean but can't lock it in. As a panel member behind closed doors were instructed to only mark off and give credit for it being verbalized. We can't assume what you meant or give the benefit of the doubt.

With the scenarios I've provided make sure you record the answers. Play them back and be your own panel assessor. Listen to yourself articulate the responses and rate your responses. Are they clear and concise? Did you utilize resources properly? Did you de-escalate the scene? Did you provide services to your troops, suspects family, and yourself? Yes, did you take the opportunity to take advantage of self care? These are the fine details that will separate you from the pack.

If you missed any of the possible answers don't get frustrated. This is completely normal and with practice and a strong dedication to your study regimen you can nail it.

Promotional processes are more about mastering the testing process than the actual substance in them. Going into a promotional process and knowing how you're being accessed and how to master that is a major advantage over your competition. While your fellow co-workers are burning the midnight oil studying department general orders and charge codes you should be zeroing in on detail verbalization.

Notice in this book we discussed nothing about case law, charge codes, elements of offenses, or department general orders? There are several reasons for this. If you're putting in for a promotional process one would like to think you know what the fourth amendment is and how search and seizure works (Please tell me you know…). Department policy is great to know but not one process I've sat on or taken had a question like this; "*What is the departments policy in full on evidence collection?*" The reason being is that most agencies hire an outside company to do promotional processes. These companies advise agencies that the top things to test on are Scene management, Interpersonal Skills, Knowledge Skills and Abilities (KSA's), and attention to detail.

Most paper pusher "leaders" struggle with scenarios and practicals because they suck at verbalizing what they would do or lack any real field experience. The processes they real excel at are the administrative portions. Being able to memorize policy procedure and prioritize during in box exercises. These portions of promotional processes are very small and won’t carry your overall score.

After you take a promotional process, immediately go to the locker room or your vehicle and write down the questions or scenarios. If you need to take it again or you're taking this process for the right reason you’ll be able to pay it forward and help the next person looking to get promoted.

If your agency or the company putting the process on gives you an opportunity to do a feedback session , DO IT. Even if you scored #1, take the feedback session and I’ll tell you why. You can always improve on taking a promotional process. Just because you scored

#1 doesn't mean you knocked it out of the park. This could be an indication that everyone sucked and you were the best sucker. I don't think that's the case but it's a possibility that you don't want to gamble on. I've taken promotional processes that I knocked out of the park and went for feedback sessions and learned that areas I thought were great weren't. Your feedback administrator will actual give you information straight from the accessors.

The most important thing to remember is that you'll only get out of these promotional processes what you put into them. If you half assed studying it will show. If you do what's outlined in this book you'll give yourself an advantage. That being said, ultimately any book can give you tricks and tips but I'm not in the room with you taking the process. This about what you're going to say, say what you're thinking.

Lastly, be the future leadership that law enforcement needs. Help develop future leaders based on their hard work and skills, not hooking them up or doing them a favor. The profession already has enough managers, we need leaders. You got this! WHEN you get promoted, Don’t be an asshole!

Made in the USA
Middletown, DE
11 October 2021